18.95

S

Lucille Ball

Pioneer of Comedy

Katherine E. Krohn

Lerner Publications Company ▪ Minneapolis

To Jennifer and Lindsay

This edition of this book is available in two bindings:
Library binding by Lerner Publications Company
Soft cover by First Avenue Editions
241 First Avenue North
Minneapolis, Minnesota 55401

Copyright © 1992 by Lerner Publications Company

LIBRARY OF CONGRESS CATALOGING-IN-PUBLICATION DATA

Krohn, Katherine E.
    Lucille Ball : pioneer of comedy / Katherine E. Krohn.
        p.   cm.   — (The Achievers)
    Summary: Describes the childhood, early film career, television success, and later years of the entertainer who became a favorite sitcom character in the show "I Love Lucy."
    ISBN 0-8225-0543-6 (lib. bdg.)
    ISBN 0-8225-9603-2 (pbk.)
    1. Ball, Lucille, 1911-1989—Juvenile literature. 2. Comedians— United States—Biography—Juvenile literature. 3. Entertainers— United States—Biography—Juvenile literature. [1. Ball, Lucille, 1911-1989. 2. Entertainers.] I. Title. II. Series.
PN2287.B16K76   1992
791.45'028'092—dc20
[B]   91-24757
                                                                   CIP
                                                                    AC

Manufactured in the United States of America

1 2 3 4 5 6 7 8 9 10 01 00 99 98 97 96 95 94 93 92

Contents

Lucille Ball and Desi Arnaz were partners on and off the television screen.

6

1
Candy Capers

One by one, chocolate candies crept down the conveyor belt toward Lucy and Ethel. Their job at Kramer's Kandy Kitchen was to wrap each piece of candy as it went past them on the belt. Lucy smiled at her friend Ethel and confidently twisted a cellophane wrapper around one of the fresh chocolates. The job seemed simple!

But then the supervisor yelled, "Speed it up!" and the candy raced along the conveyor belt at high speed. The chocolates started to pile up and slip away, unwrapped. In a panic, Lucy crammed candy into her mouth until her cheeks were bulging. Lucy's eyes looked like they would pop out of her head.

Television's most famous redhead was in trouble again. Lucy Ricardo and Ethel Mertz were very close to losing the bet they had made with their husbands, Ricky and Fred, that they could hold down jobs.

The classic candy factory scene

And the boss at the factory was soon to discover that Lucy and Ethel had absolutely no experience as candy wrappers, as they had claimed in their job interview.

To hide their mistakes, Lucy and Ethel even stuffed the unwrapped candy down their blouses and inside their floppy chef hats—creating one of the funniest moments in the history of television.

As usual, Lucy would find her way out of this particular mess. And, as always, TV viewers would be swept away with Lucy in a typically hilarious adventure.

I Love Lucy, the situation comedy that made a talented film actress named Lucille Ball into an all-time favorite television star, first aired on CBS on October 15, 1951. The show featured Lucy's real-life husband, Desi Arnaz, as glamorous Cuban band-leader, Ricky Ricardo. Lucille Ball played his lively wife, Lucy.

Characters Fred and Ethel Mertz, portrayed by William Frawley and Vivian Vance, also appeared regularly on the show. The Mertzes were the Ricardos' best friends, downstairs neighbors, and landlords.

Lucy was known for her wild imagination and her goofy schemes. She would do things that most people would not dream of doing—stomp grapes with her bare feet, take a pie in the face, or even walk the ledge of a skyscraper. One writer observed, "She would do anything to get what she wanted. That's why we loved her. She was gutsy."

A homemaker on the show, Lucy's dream was to have a show-business career. Husband Ricky wanted Lucy to be an ordinary housewife, but Lucy wanted much more.

Many *I Love Lucy* plots involved Lucy's sneaky attempts to break into show business. She frequently begged Ricky to introduce her to his celebrity friends, and sometimes she would make herself an unwelcome addition to one of Ricky's nightclub acts.

Other plots involved a bet or a challenge between the women and the men. Lucy often talked Ethel into joining one of her schemes to prove a point to Ricky. Likewise, Ricky and Fred often teamed up to teach their wives a lesson.

Some episodes featured Lucy and Ricky struggling with the everyday conflicts of married life. Television audiences everywhere could relate to this theme.

I Love Lucy plots usually started out being believable. After that, the show started to get silly and absurd. "There's always a smooth transition from sense to nonsense," explained a TV reviewer, "not just unbelievable slapstick from start to finish."

In the classic "Lucy Does a TV Commercial," Lucy is hired to do a live TV advertisement for a health tonic called Vitameatavegamin. The commercial, in which Lucy samples a spoonful of the tonic, has to be filmed several times. Gradually, Lucy gets drunk on Vitameatavegamin, which is 23 percent alcohol. Barely able to stand up, let alone say her lines, Lucy blurts, "Are you unpoopular? Do you pop out at parties?"

Opposite: Lucy pitches Vitameatavegamin. Sometimes Lucy didn't even have to say a word, her face said it all.

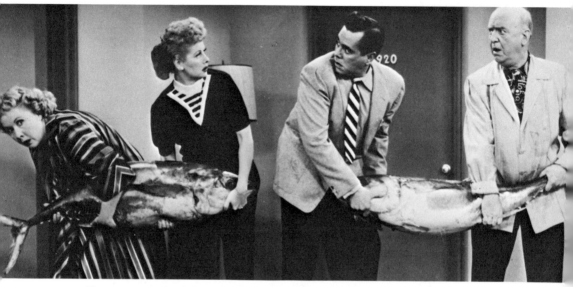

The women and the men made a bet on who could catch the bigger fish. These big ones were "caught" at a fish store.

Early critics of *I Love Lucy* said the show would never last. They said viewers would not believe that an American woman would be married to a Cuban man. "What do you mean no one will believe it?" asked Lucy. "We are married!" She refused to do the show without husband Desi.

As the show grew in popularity, Lucy became a role model for other actresses. A trend called "Lucillism" spread across Hollywood as TV directors tried to make actresses be more like Lucy. Of course, being Lucylike only worked for Lucy. She had her own unique personality and performing style.

I Love Lucy was produced by Lucy and Desi's company, Desilu Productions. Desilu became famous for breaking new ground in TV broadcasting. Most other TV shows of the early 1950s were broadcast live—that is, viewers would watch a program on television at the same time the show was being performed in the studio. Many of these early shows were never seen again because they weren't captured on film. But *I Love Lucy* was prerecorded on film, so episodes could be broadcast again and again.

Desilu used the "three-camera technique" to film the *I Love Lucy* show. With this method, which is still commonly used to tape television programs, a central camera filmed the scene head-on, and side cameras shot detailed close-ups of the actors from different angles. The different shots were then edited together to create the final show.

Another Desilu technique that would become a TV standard was the use of a live audience. Lucy insisted that she could perform better when she could hear an audience's reaction. So, from the very first show, she and Desi provided 300 seats in the studio for a live audience.

Before each of the 179 half-hour *I Love Lucy* episodes and 13 hour-long specials, Desi would step in front of the audience and welcome everyone to the show. Then the actors would find their places, and the show would begin.

"If I had to use one word to describe Lucy, it would be 'energy,'" a movie executive said.

I Love Lucy ran for six television seasons and left a lasting TV legacy. In 1984 Lucille Ball was inducted into the Academy of Television Arts and Sciences Hall of Fame. In 1991 Desi Arnaz joined the TV Hall of Fame, as did the *I Love Lucy* show itself— the first series ever inducted.

I Love Lucy reruns are still shown around the world, and the show is even broadcast in several languages. In many cities in the United States, you can see Lucy two or three times a day. It is said that at any given moment, someone, somewhere is watching Lucy on television.

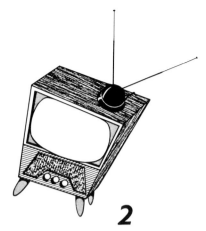

2
Dramatic Entrance

Lucille Desiree Ball was born on August 6, 1911, in Jamestown, in western New York state. Soon after Lucy was born, she moved with her parents, Desiree (DeDe) and Henry Ball, to Anaconda, Montana, where Lucy's father took a job as a telephone lineman.

Within a year, however, the Balls left Montana. The Michigan Telephone Company offered Henry a job at better pay, and the family moved to Wyandotte, Michigan, a small industrial town near Detroit.

It wasn't long after the move to Wyandotte that tragedy struck. Henry Ball caught typhoid fever and became so sick that he could no longer work. He lost his job at the telephone company, and the city's health department put a big sign on the Balls' front door that read: "KEEP OUT—HEALTH AUTHORITIES." The Balls' friends and neighbors were afraid they would catch typhoid fever and stayed far away from the house. Henry's health grew worse. On February 15, 1915, Henry Ball passed away.

At the time, DeDe was four months pregnant with her second child. She decided it would be best to return to her hometown in New York, so she could be close to relatives when the new baby was born. DeDe and Lucy moved in with DeDe's parents, Fred and Florabelle Hunt, who lived in the town of Celoron, near Jamestown. There, Lucy's brother, Frederick (Freddie), was born.

From an early age, Lucy seemed to have a way of getting in and out of trouble. Her flair for dramatics was contagious. Lucy loved to pull the neighborhood kids into kooky schemes and dramas. She liked to make up plays, and she even turned her grandparents' chicken coop into a stage.

Grandpa Hunt liked to take Lucy and her brother Freddie on fun adventures, like crack-of-dawn fishing trips and expeditions to pick wild mushrooms. Grandpa Hunt also introduced Lucy to the world of theater. Lucy, Freddie, and Grandpa Hunt regularly rode the five-cent streetcar into nearby Jamestown to see the latest vaudeville acts.

Vaudeville was a popular form of entertainment in the early 1900s. Vaudeville shows consisted of a variety of separate performances by singers, musicians, comedians, and acrobats. Lucy loved the madcap humor of vaudeville. The shows influenced her emerging talents in a profound way.

Observing the comedians, Lucy learned how to

deliver a punch line and how to pull off a joke by making expressive gestures and faces. Lucy also learned that *she* wanted to make people laugh. She understood how humor could lift people out of their everyday lives to a place where they could be silly and forget their problems for a while.

DeDe, Freddie, and Lucy in 1915

Lucy's childhood home in Celoron, New York

When Lucy was nine, her mother remarried. Lucy's new stepfather, Ed Peterson, introduced Lucy to the theater community in nearby Chautauqua, New York, a hot spot for exciting new actors and musicians. There, Lucy saw a monologist—a lone actor on a bare stage—"creating a whole world out of nothing, making people laugh and cry."

"It was magic," Lucy said.

Lucy's interest in drama continued into high school. She joined the school drama club and acted in several plays, including *Charley's Aunt.* "I played the lead, directed it, cast it, sold the tickets, printed the posters, and hauled furniture to the school for scenery and props," she recalled.

Lucy was also involved in basketball, softball, and cheerleading in high school, though she was never an outstanding athlete. DeDe was a talented pianist and she gave Lucy her first music lessons. "I wasn't very good in music, but I played piano, ukulele, and saxophone," Lucy once said with her usual modesty. She even studied at a well-respected music school for a short time.

Lucy earned good grades in school but sometimes had trouble concentrating. Teachers were perplexed that a bright student like Lucy so frequently stared into space.

More than likely, Lucy was making plans for her future as an actress and imagining the glamorous life she would lead as a celebrity. Lucy recalled, "I would excuse myself from class to get a drink of water and never come back. I'd start walking toward New York City and keep walking until someone brought me home."

Always eager to work, Lucy held part-time jobs throughout much of her youth. She carefully saved her earnings and planned for her future. When Lucy was 16, DeDe gave Lucy permission to drop out of high school and enroll in the acclaimed John Murray Anderson/Robert Milton School of the Theater and Dance in New York City.

Lucy was more than ready to begin her life as an actress when she boarded the bus to New York.

3
Casting Off

Seated behind wrought-iron gates and resembling an elegant southern mansion, the Anderson/Milton School at 128-130 East Fifty-eighth Street in New York City had a look of seriousness and importance. Classes were conducted with a similar seriousness. Students couldn't speak without permission from the instructor, and no one could miss a class except for illness. The school was very expensive, and it offered challenging courses taught by some of the best drama instructors in the country.

Newly enrolled in the school, Lucy took on a full schedule. She had a wide range of interesting classes to choose from, such as basic drama, motion-picture acting, musical-comedy acting, play writing, stage direction and management, and costume design.

The now-legendary actress Bette Davis was one of Lucy's classmates. Even as a teenager, Bette was self-confident and extremely talented.

Bette Davis would emerge as a great film star of the '30s and '40s, while Lucy would find her fame on the TV screen years later.

Unlike Bette, Lucy was very shy. Performing for friends and family in Celoron had been easy. But Lucy became nervous in front of her demanding teachers and confident classmates. She had a hard time just speaking up in class. One of the acting teachers sent an angry telegram to Lucy's mother that declared, "Lucy has no talent." The instructor also said that Lucy was "wasting her money."

Unsure what steps to take next, Lucy moved home. But soon she begged her mother to let her go back to New York City. She would room with friends and try her luck again.

DeDe wasn't thrilled with Lucy's decision. But DeDe believed in allowing her children the freedom to express themselves, and she wanted Lucy to be happy. DeDe knew Lucy would only be happy as an actress.

Because she had little acting experience, Lucy knew it wouldn't be easy to get work in vaudeville or a role in a play. She decided to become a show girl. Lots of musical shows needed chorus girls, and Lucy was a fairly good dancer. Even as an unknown dancer, she would be seen by the public.

One day Lucy was reading a newspaper, and she saw an advertisement for an upcoming audition. The musical *Rio Rita* needed chorus girls, and Lucy rushed to the theatre. Her enthusiasm paid off — she was given a part in the show. But soon after rehearsals began, Lucy was fired.

Lucy wasn't sure why she had lost the job. She thought perhaps she wasn't glamorous enough, so she changed her name to Diane Belmont, hoping to improve her image. But this change didn't help her.

During the next few months, Lucy landed several other chorus girl parts. But in a series of disappointments, she was fired from each job. With no formal dance training, Lucy just didn't measure up. She realized that she would have to work harder if she wanted a show-business career. "I couldn't sing. I couldn't dance. I didn't know how to act," Lucy later joked. "Nobody told me you needed talent to be an actress!"

Lucy wasn't ready to give up—she decided to become a model. She worked as a part-time secretary and a department store clerk and took modeling classes in her off-hours. Lucy didn't have to wait long to get her first modeling assignment. She was chosen to pose as the "Chesterfield Girl" for the cigarette company's billboard advertisements. Lucy's face was soon plastered on billboards all over New York City.

The billboard exposure led Lucy to a modeling job with a famous dress designer, Hattie Carnegie, who made clothes for many of Hollywood's greatest actresses. Lucy liked the job, but she didn't think she fit in with the other glamorous models. "I always felt like an outsider," Lucy once said.

To keep her figure slim, Lucy resorted to a near-starvation diet. One day, her poor eating habits and stressful schedule caught up with her. She collapsed during a fashion show at the Carnegie studio.

Hattie Carnegie helped Lucy up off the floor and rushed her to a hospital. Doctors determined that the muscles in Lucy's legs were damaged and that she might never walk again.

Lucy had once been injured in a automobile accident and her legs had never completely healed. After the accident, Lucy developed painful arthritis in her legs. The stress of modeling and the long hours of standing and posing, together with Lucy's poor diet, had severely strained her weak legs.

Lucy had no choice but to return home to Celoron. Bedridden and nearly crippled, Lucy never gave up hope that she would walk again. Her mother shared her faith and massaged Lucy's slow-healing legs morning and night.

It took nearly two years for Lucy to recover. Eventually, she moved around on crutches, and then she walked with a cane. At age 21, Lucy had to learn how to walk all over again.

By the spring of 1933, Lucy was finally back to her former self. Her legs were strong and so was her desire to go back to New York. She returned to her modeling job at Carnegie, but her mind was still set on being an actress.

One morning Lucy ran into a casting agent who was desperately trying to find a show girl for an MGM movie. A dancer had backed out at the last minute, and the agent thought Lucy would be ideal for the part.

MGM producer Sam Goldwyn required that all his chorus girls have public exposure on billboard signs. Lucy's experience as a Chesterfield Girl won her the job. But she'd have to leave for Hollywood immediately.

Lucy, having shed her stage name of Diane Belmont, packed her bags for Hollywood. She was thrilled to be appearing in her first film—an MGM musical called *Roman Scandals*, starring comedian and singer Eddie Cantor.

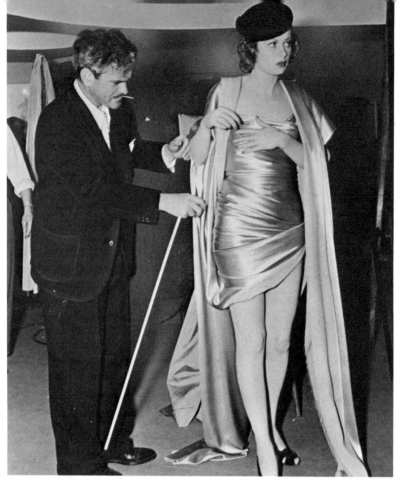

Lucy's training as a model paid off throughout her acting career.

While performing in *Roman Scandals*, Lucy forced herself to overcome her shyness. She clowned with everyone on the set and even charmed the director into giving her one line of dialogue.

For the first time in Lucy's acting career, her work was appreciated. She was asked to stay on as a chorus girl at MGM. As a "Goldwyn Girl," Lucy earned what seemed like an enormous salary at the time—$150 a week. Her chorus roles were minor, but important people in the entertainment industry were beginning to take notice. Lucy would take her occasional line of dialogue and give it all she had. Sometimes she would arrive late to rehearsals—just so the director would notice her.

While working at MGM, Lucy made a big change in her appearance. One day the studio hairstylist hovered over Lucy and proclaimed, "The hair is brown, but the soul is on fire!" He then dyed Lucy's hair the fiery orange color that would become her trademark.

Lucy stayed on at MGM for nearly a year and learned a great deal about acting in films. She also decided she didn't want to be cast as a show girl forever. Eventually, she left MGM and signed on at Columbia Pictures.

At Columbia, Lucy was assigned a variety of bit parts, mostly in westerns and comedies. She found the roles to be unchallenging. In *Room Service*, the Marx brothers hurled pies at Lucy's face. In *Three Little Pigskins*, the Three Stooges squirted her with seltzer water.

The job at Columbia was short-lived. The studio was having financial problems and had to fire most of its actors, including Lucy. The news was awful.

Lucy had just invited her whole family to come live with her in Hollywood, thinking her acting career was finally secure. The family arrived on the very day that Lucy lost her job at Columbia—and she didn't want to send them back home. She found temporary work at Paramount Pictures as a film "extra," an actor who appears anonymously in a group scene.

As an extra in the 1935 film *Roberta*, starring dancers Fred Astaire and Ginger Rogers, Lucy played a model in a fashion show. In one scene, she gracefully descended a staircase in a white satin dress and a white ostrich-feather cape—just the way Hattie Carnegie had taught her. The head of RKO Studios, Pandro Berman, happened to see the scene. Berman was very impressed—he offered Lucy a seven-year contract with RKO. Lucy knew this was a great opportunity.

As a contract player at RKO, Lucy played whatever role the particular director thought was suitable. "If they wanted a dance-hall hostess, you were a dance-hall hostess. If they wanted a nun, you were a nun," explained Lucy.

In the 1940 film *Too Many Girls*, Lucy played a spoiled heiress named Connie Casey. Connie's father hires four football players to protect his daughter when she goes off to college. One of Lucy's on-screen body-guards was to change her life. His name was Desi Arnaz.

Desiderio Alberto Arnaz III was best known at the time for his real-life role as the leader of a rumba dance band. Desi was handsome and charming, and he loved to tell jokes with his thick Cuban accent.

Desi and Lucy in the film *Forever Darling*

Actress Ann Miller introduced Lucy to Desi in the RKO cafeteria one day at lunchtime, a few days before Lucy and Desi were to begin working together in *Too Many Girls*. "It was like love at first sight," Ann observed. "When I introduced her to him, her eyes just lit up. He was the cutest thing around."

Lucy made quite a first impression on Desi, too. She was still in costume for a part she was playing as a hotheaded show girl in *Dance, Girl, Dance*. She greeted Desi in a slinky dress, a messy wig, and a fake black eye.

"I didn't like her at first," Desi remembered. "She looked awful. Very tough." Later that day, Desi saw Lucy again. She was wearing a yellow skirt and a cashmere sweater and she looked completely different. Desi was smitten and he offered to teach Lucy to rumba.

By the time *Too Many Girls* was completed, Lucy and Desi had fallen in love. They kept in touch by telephone as Desi toured the country with his band. Six months later, they decided to get married.

Lucy's friends warned her not to marry Desi. He was six years younger than Lucy, and her friends felt he was too flashy and wild. But on November 30, 1940, in Greenwich, Connecticut, Lucy and Desi were wed by a justice of the peace in a spur-of-the-moment ceremony. Desi gave Lucy a cheap dimestore ring that he'd picked up at the last minute. It would fill in until Desi could buy Lucy a real wedding ring.

Even Lucy was unsure about the marriage. "I took the plunge because I loved him," Lucy said. "It was the most daring thing I ever did. Hollywood gave our marriage six months, I gave it six weeks!"

Lucy charmed movie and TV fans with her brilliant blue eyes, flaming red hair, and "bow-tie" mouth.

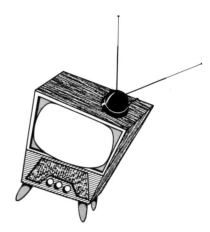

4
Prime Time

Lucy waved to Desi from her car as they passed each other on Sepulveda Boulevard in Los Angeles. At five o'clock on a Monday morning, the newlyweds were driving in completely different directions.

With more than 40 films already to her credit, Lucy was on her way to work at RKO Studios. Desi was exhausted after a long night of leading his band at a nearby nightclub. "We would pull off the road and talk for a few minutes," Lucy recalled. "That's a dull way to live!"

In the early 1940s, Lucy appeared in a variety of films—both dramas and comedies. In 1942 she landed her first major dramatic role at RKO, playing a crippled girl in *The Big Street*. Perhaps because she herself had been crippled, Lucy could play the part with sincerity and feeling. A critic wrote at the time, "Lucille Ball tackles her emotional role as if it were sirloin and she didn't care who was looking."

Although she earned favorable reviews as a dramatic actress, Lucy was not a box-office superstar. Fortunately, her career continued to take her in new directions. In the days before television, people tuned into weekly radio shows just as we follow our favorite TV programs. In 1946, Lucy began work on a CBS Radio comedy called *My Favorite Husband*. In a hint of things to come, she played a klutzy homemaker on the popular show.

In *My Favorite Husband* Lucy began to prove that she was more than just a stock dramatic actress. Lucy had a gift for comedy. As Lucy's popularity grew steadily, Desi continued to tour the country with his band. But marriage-by-telephone was not only expensive, it was tearing the couple apart.

Lucy and Desi knew they needed to see more of each other if their marriage was going to last, so they decided to work together. They created a musical comedy act called "Desi Arnaz and Band with Lucille Ball." Lucy and Desi wrote most of the skits and jokes themselves and set out across the country on a 12-week tour.

When the tour ended, Lucy was sure she wanted to continue working with Desi. She went to see her business manager and said, "Unless Desi and I can act together in the future, I will never act again."

Meanwhile, people all over the United States were buying their first television sets. It was the early 1950s, and television was a new industry. It created many jobs for actors, writers, and production people.

Lucy wasted no time plunging into the new field. She was offered a leading role in a CBS television program that would be based on *My Favorite Husband*. Still, Lucy had hesitations. If the show wasn't a success, it could damage her film career. But she decided to take a chance.

Lucy's mom, DeDe, liked to visit Lucy in the film studio.

CBS network executives wanted Lucy's radio costar, Richard Denning, to play her TV husband. Lucy liked working with Denning, but she was convinced that Desi should play her on-screen husband. She argued with the executives until she got her way. Then, at the last moment, the show's commercial sponsor (the company that put up the money to produce the show) backed out of the agreement.

The company thought viewers would not accept the idea of an American woman being married to a Cuban man, and it didn't want to sponsor a show that might fail. Suddenly, without money to produce the program, production came to a stop.

Desi and Lucy were upset. But they were determined not to give up. They decided to form their own production company. The couple borrowed $8,000 and, with another $8,000 of their own, formed Desilu Productions. Now Desi and Lucy could make the kind of show they really wanted.

The couple looked all over Los Angeles to find a suitable building to house their new production company. They found an old, run-down film studio, hired a construction crew, and turned the place into an impressive television studio.

The crew hurriedly built sets and props, put in electrical wiring and lighting, and constructed bleacher seats for the audience. The studio was renamed "The Desilu Playhouse."

At this crucial point, Desi and Lucy and their talented crew made decisions that would set the standards for the new field of television production. Desi explained, "We had no rules to go by, so we made them up."

Bigoted advertisers didn't want a Cuban man to play Lucy's TV husband. So Lucy and Desi started their own company and produced the *I Love Lucy* show their way.

Vivian Vance and William Frawley were better known to TV viewers as Ethel and Fred Mertz.

Desi and Lucy hired scriptwriters Madelyn Pugh, Bob Carroll, Jr., and Jess Oppenheimer. Oppenheimer also became the show's producer. Lucy was very familiar with his work—Jess Oppenheimer had served as the producer and writer on *My Favorite Husband* for three years.

Lucy and Desi no longer wanted to transfer *My Favorite Husband* directly to television. The writers created a new cast of characters and a "pilot" script.

They wanted to get a test audience's reaction to the show before it would be shown on national television.

In the pilot episode, Lucy and Desi played Lucy and Larry Lopez, characters who closely resembled their real-life personalities. Larry was a successful bandleader, and Lucy was a movie star.

The test audience liked the pilot show, as did Lucy and Desi's new commercial sponsor, Philip Morris Cigarettes. But the audience felt the lead characters should be more like everyday people instead of famous celebrities.

So the writers put their pens to work again and created Lucy and Ricky Ricardo. Ricky remained a bandleader, but Lucy went from movie star to imaginative homemaker.

The Ricardos lived in a simple brownstone apartment, number 4-A, at 623 East Sixty-sixth Street in New York City. (According to real New York geography, the apartment would actually be in the middle of New York's East River!) The new show was crowned *I Love Lucy*.

Desi took on the task of finding cast members and quickly hired William Frawley to play the grumpy landlord, Fred Mertz. But Desi had a more difficult time choosing the actress who would play the part of Fred's wife, Ethel. Just days before the first show was to be filmed, Desi discovered stage actress Vivian Vance performing in a southern California playhouse.

Desi had a hunch she would be perfect for the role of Ethel.

Vivian had a special rule in her contract. As long as she played Ethel, she had to remain 20 pounds (9 kilograms) overweight. The director wanted Ethel Mertz to appear frumpier and older than Lucy Ricardo. In reality, Lucille Ball was one year older than Vivian Vance.

The preparations for the show were hectic. Lucy had to attend to thousands of details. But she also had her own personal concerns. She was pregnant. On July 17, 1951, just six weeks before the first *I Love Lucy* show was to be filmed, Lucy gave birth to her first child, Lucie Desiree Arnaz.

Desi and Lucy had wanted a child for many years and were extremely happy about the baby. Lucy stayed at home for a few weeks, but then was called to her role as Lucy Ricardo.

"The Girls Want to Go to a Nightclub" was the first *I Love Lucy* episode broadcast to a national audience. In this show, Fred and Ethel cannot decide how to celebrate their 18th wedding anniversary. Ethel wants a romantic night of dinner and dancing at the Copacabana Nightclub. Fred wants to go to a boxing match. Soon Lucy gets involved, and the Mertzes' minor disagreement turns into a major fiasco—with hilarious results. *I Love Lucy* quickly became the most talked-about TV show in the country.

It looks like Lucy has lost her head. As usual, Ethel is on hand to help bail Lucy out of trouble.

In the spring of 1952, as the first *I Love Lucy* season was drawing to a close, Lucy discovered she was expecting another baby. Lucy was worried. She feared her pregnancy might hurt the show's ratings and put a stop to production. She was terrified to tell Jess Oppenheimer that she was pregnant.

But, to Lucy's surprise, Oppenheimer laughed and his eyes lit up when she gave him the news. "Boy, what a gimmick!" he said. "In the show we'll have Lucy Ricardo pregnant, too!"

Lucy wrestles with a professional grape stomper in the messiest
I Love Lucy episode of all time.

This was the first time a pregnant actress would play a pregnant woman on television. Although this was a television breakthrough, the scriptwriters had to be very careful about censorship rules. In the 1950s, some people thought pregnancy was an inappropriate subject for television.

During the course of Lucy's pregnancy, every single *I Love Lucy* script had to pass the careful inspection of a rabbi, a priest, and a minister before it could be broadcast on television. The writers referred to Lucy as "expectant," fearing that viewers would be offended by the word "pregnant."

In "Lucy Is Enceinte" (*enceinte* is the French word for pregnant), Lucy finds a special way to break the news to Ricky that she is expecting a baby. Lucy goes out for the evening to the Tropicana, Ricky's nightclub. Sitting at a table near the stage, Lucy secretly slips a note to her waiter, who later gives it to Ricky. Soon, Ricky reads the note to the audience: "My husband and I are going to have a blessed event, and I just found out today. I've heard you sing 'We're Having a Baby.' Would you sing it for us?"

Ricky grins and graciously agrees to sing the song. First, he sings the classic lullaby, "Rockabye Baby," winding his way through the different tables in the nightclub, stopping to ask each couple if they are the ones expecting the baby. Each couple shakes their heads "no." Finally, Ricky arrives at Lucy's table. He continues to sing the lullaby, while Lucy nods a shy "yes." Ricky looks at her in disbelief and then, understanding suddenly, sings "We're Having a Baby" to his wife.

Vivian Vance remembered, "The night they filmed the show in which Lucy tells Ricky about the baby coming, everybody on the set started crying. Lucy cried, Desi cried, even the prop men cried. They were all so teary-eyed that we were going to do retakes and the audience yelled 'No!' It was all perfect."

The following series of shows focused on Lucy's pregnancy. In the segment filmed November 7, 1952,

"Lucy Becomes a Sculptress," Lucy takes sculpting classes in hopes her unborn child will have artistic leanings.

In "Ricky Has Labor Pains," Ricky complains of "morning sickness," until the doctor determines that Ricky is just feeling left out because Lucy and the unborn baby are getting so much attention. Ricky quickly recovers when the doctor prescribes a "daddy shower" to be attended by all of Ricky's buddies.

Lucy and Desi were hoping to have a baby boy, so it was written into the script that the Ricardos' child would be a boy. Lucy and her doctor decided to deliver the baby by a surgical method called a Caesarean section. That way, Lucy and Desi could choose the exact day the baby would be born. They chose Monday, January 19, 1953, as the birth date.

The birth of the TV baby would be broadcast on the same day, but the show would be filmed several weeks ahead of time. Lucy would be able to get plenty of rest before the birth of her real baby.

Lucille Ball gave birth to a son, Desiderio Alberto Arnaz IV, two hours before Lucy Ricardo gave birth to her son "Little Ricky" on *I Love Lucy*. Forty million fans (one in four Americans) watched "Lucy Goes to the Hospital." More viewers watched this single *I Love Lucy* episode than tuned in for the inauguration of President Dwight Eisenhower or the coronation of the Queen of England, broadcast in the same year.

Newspapers worldwide carried front-page headlines announcing the birth of Desi, Jr. More than 30,000 fans sent congratulation cards. Baby booties arrived by the truckload. And there were so many flowers in Lucy's hospital room that the nurses and doctors had a hard time making their way to Lucy's bedside.

Soon after Desi, Jr., was born, Lucy received her first two Emmy Awards from the Academy of Television Arts and Sciences. Lucy was named Best Comedienne, and *I Love Lucy* took top honors as the year's Best Situation Comedy. Lucy and Desi also signed a record-breaking contract with their sponsor. They would receive $8 million over the next 2½ years to continue playing Lucy and Ricky Ricardo.

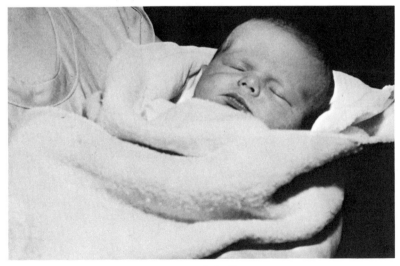

"Little Ricky"

Several child actors played the part of Little Ricky. The most well known was Keith Thibodeaux.

Lucy had arrived at the most exciting point in her career. She was famous and very wealthy. She had the leading role as TV's favorite funnywoman. But behind Lucy's well-known face was a very real human being. Lucy had her share of problems.

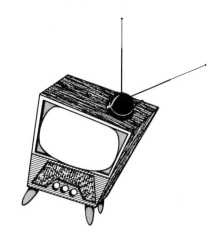

5
Red Scare

The 1950s were a somewhat fearful and cautious time in the United States. A few powerful politicians were very worried that the Communist political party would take over the country. These politicians, led by Senator Joseph McCarthy, formed the Un-American Activities Committee in the House of Representatives and called suspected Communists to trial.

Some organizations "blacklisted," or refused to hire, alleged Communists. Many careers were destroyed. This "red scare" affected people in Hollywood, too. Many famous entertainers—including Lucille Ball— were named as Communists.

In April 1953, Lucy was interviewed by a member of the Un-American Activities Committee. The committee had documents showing that Lucy had registered as a Communist voter in 1936. In fact, her whole family had been registered as Communist.

Lucy admitted to the committee that she *had* been registered as a Communist. But, she explained, "It was only because Grandpa Hunt wanted us to." Lucy convinced the committee that she was no longer a Communist, and if she had voted as a Communist at all, it was nearly 20 years earlier. Lucy was cleared of the charges, but only for the time being.

Lucy and Desi had just finished a very successful 1952-53 *I Love Lucy* season. They took a one-week vacation and then started work on an MGM movie, *The Long, Long Trailer*. Lucy and Desi hadn't made a film together in 11 years.

For the first time, *I Love Lucy* fans could see their favorite couple on a big screen in vivid color—instead of on a small black-and-white TV set. In fact, *The Long, Long Trailer* was the first film to star famous TV personalities.

Much of the movie was filmed in Yosemite National Park in California. There, fans gathered to catch a glimpse of the popular TV stars. One magazine reported, "When Lucy and Desi went to lunch, it took ten cops to get them through the crowds."

Lucy and Desi played newlyweds Tacy and Nicky Collini who take a trip across the country, hauling a huge new trailer home behind their car. The trip proves to be nothing but trouble.

In one scene, Tacy tries to save time by whipping up dinner in the trailer, while Nicky continues to drive the car to a trailer park. The trailer kitchen receives a thorough shaking—with Tacy trapped inside. Drawers and cabinets swing open, and pots, pans, and food go flying. When Nicky finally pulls over, Tacy stumbles out of the trailer, completely covered in flour.

Nicky Collini tries to park the long, long trailer.

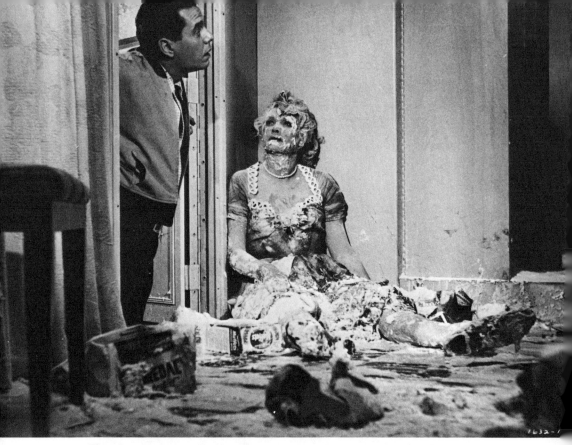

The *Long, Long Trailer* flour scene. Lucy made her TV and movie antics look easy, but she was often sore for days after filming a slapstick routine.

In *The Long, Long Trailer*, Lucy and Desi used many of the comic devices that worked so well for them on television. The film was a big box-office success, and it boosted *I Love Lucy*'s already high ratings.

At summer's end, Lucy and Desi started back to work on a new *I Love Lucy* season. They rehearsed four days a week at the studio. On the fifth day, they filmed the show.

I Love Lucy was a true team effort, on and off the set. In the studio, Lucy took charge of the creative end of the show. She demanded that every scene be flawless—down to the tiniest detail. Lucy would rehearse a difficult stunt over and over again until it was perfect. She required the same perfection from each member of the cast and crew.

While Lucy handled the creative details, Desi made most of the show's business decisions. On the air, Lucy and Desi were also a well-matched comic team. As Ricky Ricardo, Desi would play the "straight man" to Lucy's comic stunts. He would frequently stand by in disbelief as Lucy's half-baked schemes turned into full-blown disasters.

Sometimes, minor disagreements between husband and wife would end in all-out battles, with Ricky losing his patience and starting to yell—in Spanish— or Lucy giving Ricky the silent treatment. The fights were funny, especially since the couple always made up at the show's end.

But Lucy and Desi also fought when the cameras weren't rolling. And these fights didn't always have a happy ending. Tempers flared and relations were often tense on the *I Love Lucy* set.

To make matters worse, Lucy's political beliefs were called into question once more. On September 4, 1953, Lucy was again interviewed by an investigator from the Un-American Activities Committee. The

Los Angeles Herald Express carried the headline: "LUCILLE BALL NAMED RED," while newspapers around the nation covered the story. Lucy's reputation and career (and the future of Desilu) were in severe danger.

Despite her worries, Lucy prepared for the weekly production of *I Love Lucy* as normal. On the day the show was to be filmed, all of the 300 seats in the Desilu Playhouse were taken. Many seats were filled by journalists who wanted to know how the general public felt about Lucy, now that she was again accused of being a Communist.

As always, Desi stepped out to greet the audience before the show. But this time he had a special speech to make. He told the audience that Lucy was very patriotic and that she was a devoted American. Then he said, "And now I want you to meet my wife—my favorite redhead—in fact, that's the only thing red about her, and even that's not real!"

When Lucy took the stage, the audience cheered and gave her a standing ovation. It wasn't long before Lucy was completely cleared of charges that she was a Communist.

Although this crisis was past, there was still tension on the *I Love Lucy* set. Lucy and Desi had a successful TV show, two loving children, and a famous television production company. But their marriage had been far from perfect.

Lucy and Desi began to argue more frequently. It was becoming harder and harder for them to work together. Despite the deep love between them, their marriage was coming apart.

Ricky scolds Lucy, who's trying to smuggle 25 pounds of Italian cheese (disguised as a baby) home to her mother.

6
Leave 'Em Laughing

After the fall of 1957, Desilu stopped producing weekly *I Love Lucy* episodes. Viewers could still watch *I Love Lucy* reruns (which were shown during prime time), and the cast members came together to produce an occasional *Lucy-Desi Comedy Hour* special.

The very last hour-long special, "The Redhead Meets the Mustache," was filmed on March 2, 1960. For the final time, Lucy Ricardo put on a disguise to sneak into the company of a celebrity. This time, Lucy wore a fake mustache and posed as a chauffeur for comedian Ernie Kovacs.

On-screen, Lucy was as funny as ever. But off-camera, she wasn't laughing—she wasn't even smiling. After nine years of hard work to create one of the most successful and memorable programs ever seen on television, the whole crew of *I Love Lucy* was saying goodbye.

But Lucy wasn't just saying goodbye to her friends on the set, her job, or the fictional Ricardos. She knew her marriage to Desi was almost over. An onlooker remembered, "Every time they wanted to film a funny scene, Lucy would break down and cry. Nobody could stand to watch it."

The day after the last show was filmed, Lucy filed for a divorce from Desi. Despite years as a successful professional team, Lucy and Desi knew they had to separate.

Years later, Desi Arnaz, Jr., reflected, "I learned pretty early to relate to *I Love Lucy* as a TV show and to my parents as actors in it. There wasn't much relationship between what I saw on TV and what was going on at home. Those were difficult years— all those funny things happening each week on television to people who looked like my parents, then the same people agonizing through some terrible, unhappy times at home."

Lucy was depressed after her divorce, but she decided to go right back to work. She made a movie called *The Facts of Life* with her good friend Bob Hope. After completing that project, she took the lead role in a Broadway play—a musical called *Wildcat*. In her first singing role, Lucy played a tough cowgirl who goes looking for oil in hopes of making it rich.

While Lucy was in New York performing in *Wildcat*, some friends talked about a man they wanted Lucy to meet. Lucy wasn't in the mood for romance after her recent divorce. "I put it off two or three times," she explained. "Finally one night I was hungry and I said, 'Well, I'll go for something to eat.'" Over a pizza, Lucy was introduced to nightclub comedian Gary Morton. Less than a year later, on November 19, 1961, she married him.

After her role in *Wildcat*, which she considered to be one of her worst performances, Lucy was eager to return to television. She launched a brand-new television series, *The Lucy Show*. Instead of Lucy Ricardo, Lucy played Lucy Carmichael, a widow and mother of two young children.

Lucie, Desi, Jr., Gary Morton, and Lucy in 1965

Lucy went all the way to Connecticut to talk her good friend Vivian Vance into costarring on the show. Since leaving her nine-year role as Ethel Mertz, Vivian had remarried and moved away from Hollywood. With a little prodding, she agreed to costar in *The Lucy Show*—but only if her character's name could be Viv, instead of Ethel. Lucy was thrilled. "I don't believe I'd have started the show without Vivian," she said.

In *The Lucy Show*, Lucy Carmichael and her children share a big house, just outside New York City, with Lucy's divorced friend Viv, who has a young son. Never before had the lives of single mothers been featured in a television comedy.

Lucy was the first female president and owner of a television studio.

Since *The Lucy Show* was a Desilu production, Desi was still involved in the project. But, a few weeks into the new show, Desi offered to sell his share of Desilu to Lucy. He wanted to go on to other projects, like raising horses on his California ranch. Lucy bought Desi's half of Desilu for $3 million.

By the 1960s, Desilu had become an enormously successful studio. In addition to *The Lucy Show,* Desilu produced *The Untouchables, The Dick Van Dyke Show, My Favorite Martian, The Andy Griffith Show*, and other TV favorites. As president of the studio, Lucy had her hands full.

The Lucy Show was on the air for six years. In 1968, Lucy formed another company, Lucille Ball Productions, and produced a new series, *Here's Lucy.* Daughter Lucie was cast as Lucy's teenage daughter. Son Desi, Jr., played Lucy's on-screen son. *Here's Lucy* lasted six years and was Lucy's last successful television series.

In 1972, while vacationing in Colorado, Lucy had a skiing accident. She broke her right leg in two places and couldn't walk for weeks. Lucy had to wear a leg brace for months and it took nearly a year for her to recover fully.

As soon as she could walk normally again, Lucy took on a very challenging role. In 1973, in the film musical *Mame*, Lucy had to perform difficult dance routines. She hadn't danced professionally in 30 years.

Lucy shares a warm greeting with actress Mary Tyler Moore. Many television comedians, including Moore, perfected their own comic routines by watching Lucy on television.

Dance instructor Onna White showed Lucy special exercises that would help strengthen the muscles in her right leg. Though "scared to death" at first, Lucy was soon dancing in *Mame*—her right leg stronger than her left.

In her later years, Lucy slowed down a bit and spent more time with her grandchildren—daughter Lucie's three children and Desi, Jr.'s, son. Lucy also liked to spend her free time cooking. Her favorite dish was green tomatoes dipped in bread crumbs and then fried.

Sometimes Lucy made public appearances at award shows. Whenever she walked onstage to present an award, she would receive a standing ovation.

While appearing on the TV game show *Password* in 1986, Lucy received the news that Desi Arnaz had died of lung cancer. With a lump in her throat, she whispered to her friend, actress Betty White, "You know, it's the darndest thing. Darn it—I didn't think I'd get this upset. There he goes."

In 1988, Lucy made her 74th film—a made-for-TV movie called *Stone Pillow*. To play the part of a homeless woman living on the streets of New York City, Lucy endured mid-summer temperatures of more than 100° F (38° C).

Lucy in *Stone Pillow*

"I was loaded down with wigs and heavy woolens and scarves and sweaters and boots," she remembered. "Not a soul, not one person said 'There's Lucy,' or 'Hello,' or 'Hi, are you Lucy?' Nobody. I was a bag lady."

Almost a year later, Lucy had a heart attack. She was hurried to a hospital, and doctors performed a complicated, high-risk operation on Lucy's damaged heart. A few days later, on April 26, 1989, Lucy passed away.

On the day Lucille Ball died, fans placed beautiful red roses on Lucy's honorary star on Hollywood Boulevard's Walk of Fame. All the flags in Lucy's home of Beverly Hills, California, were flown at half-mast.

Many would miss the very funny woman who paved the way for future generations of television performers. An acting school in Los Angeles had the perfect good-bye message for the pioneer of comedy. The sign on the school's door exclaimed, "THEY NEEDED A LAUGH IN HEAVEN. GOODBYE, LUCY."

Lucy and Jack Oakie in the 1938 film *Annabel Takes a Tour*

ACKNOWLEDGMENTS

Photographs reproduced with permission of Hollywood Book and Poster, pp. 1, 2, 8, 11, 12, 14, 46, 61; Wisconsin Center for Film and Theater Research, pp. 6, 20, 22, 30, 32, 35, 38, 41, 45, 49, 50, 54, 58, 63; *Jamestown Post-Journal*, p. 17; Fenton Historical Society, p. 18; Cleveland Public Library, pp. 26, 29, 37, 42, 53, 60, 64. Cover photographs: Wisconsin Center for Film and Theater Research.